Mindful Parenting
in a Chaotic World

EFFECTIVE STRATEGIES TO STAY
CENTERED AT HOME AND ON THE GO

Nicole Libin, PhD

**ROCKRIDGE
PRESS**

For general information on our other products and services or to obtain technical support, please contact our Customer Care Department within the United States at (866) 744-2665, or outside the United States at (510) 253-0500.

Rockridge Press publishes its books in a variety of electronic and print formats. Some content that appears in print may not be available in electronic books, and vice versa.

Interior and Cover Designer: Michael Cook
Art Producer: Sue Bischofberger
Editor: Morgan Shanahan
Production Manager: Oriana Siska
Production Editor: Melissa Edeburn

ISBN: Print 978-1-64152-892-4 | eBook 978-1-64152-925-9

For Aria and Cam:
My Lovey and my Love.
Thank you for all the things.
I love you more than all the planets,
including Pluto.

CONTENTS

INTRODUCTION

My husband and I were overjoyed when our daughter started walking. Her first steps! The joy lasted about 17 seconds before panic set in: What if she fell down the stairs or drowned in the toilet? Then she began talking, and again we were elated. Little did we know that, once she started, our perpetual noise machine would never stop. Although I was delighted by her energetic self-expression, I often felt overwhelmed, fearing I might never have a moment of quiet ever again.

Parenting brought me so many incredible joys and delights, but it also produced a stream of endless worries, tasks, and fears. I turned to mindfulness as a way to cope with this craziness. In our house, we use time-outs. But they aren't for our daughter—they're for me. When she was three and decided to cut not only her own hair but also the blinds and her books, mindfulness was my time-out. I was able to pause and take a breath when I started to lose it, which allowed me to respond with thoughtful, measured words instead of an angry tirade that I might have regretted later.

Mindfulness is the practice of paying attention to and acknowledging what's happening in your mind and body in a gentle, curious way. Being mindful allows you to choose a kinder, more accepting response to whatever arises rather than react automatically. Mindfulness doesn't make all of your stress go away. And it certainly hasn't made my kid any quieter or less rambunctious (we still haven't replaced those blinds). What mindfulness does is provide tools to help me manage my stress, so I'm less caught up in worry, less overwhelmed by fear, and more present for my daughter, my husband, and my life.

From the cover of *Time* magazine to Oprah to hundreds of smartphone apps, mindfulness is everywhere. And with good reason: A growing body of research shows that mindfulness helps regulate attention, increase self-compassion, decrease symptoms of depression and anxiety, and reduce stress. Mindfulness benefits families by increasing empathy, emotional awareness, and acceptance—who wouldn't want more of those?

Although the benefits of mindfulness are real, the common perception of it needs a serious makeover. The many images of blissfully calm people serenely meditating might lead any busy parent to dismiss mindfulness as totally unrealistic. After all, who has time to sit still when there's laundry to do or groceries to buy?

This book is an accessible, no-nonsense guide to mindfulness for busy caregivers and their families. It features

- simple, effective, and fun practices that can be done at home or on the go;

- real-life examples of how mindfulness can help the whole family;

- grounding in science, with research and neuroscience presented in straightforward language;

- a self-care focus. (As flight attendants tell us, we have to put on our own oxygen masks before helping anyone else. To truly care for our children, we need to care for ourselves.)

Caring about our kids is easy. Caring *for* them can be impossibly hard. And caring for ourselves might be the hardest challenge of all. This book is the resource I wish I had when my daughter was born—something that could provide real-world tools to help manage my overwhelming emotions (and hers) and find calmness, acceptance, and even more joy amid the chaos that we call parenting.

ALL YOU NEED IS YOU: TOOLS FOR MINDFULNESS

The number one thing to remember when practicing mindfulness is that you can't do it wrong. Everyone gets a gold star! In fact, you don't have to *do* anything at all. It's just about *being*—being you and feeling what it's like to be you, right here, right now, just as you are, and letting that be enough. You don't need to change anything or make anything happen. You don't need any fancy props or special settings. As long as you're here and breathing, you have everything you need.

Little kids are actually our best teachers for how to practice mindfulness.

Anyone who has ever tried to go for a walk with a toddler or preschooler knows that it takes forever. For the kids, there's a whole world to be with and explore—worms to watch, dirt to play in, flowers to touch and smell, cracks to jump over, and songs to sing. There's no agenda, no rush, and no problem. There are no preconceived notions or judgments about the way things should be. The children aren't comparing themselves to anyone else, thinking about all the other things they should be doing, or trying to multitask. They are in the moment, experiencing it with all of their senses. And we all know what generally happens when they get upset— the emotions, movements, and noise are epic. They feel sadness or frustration completely, with their whole bodies. There's no holding back. And then? It's gone. They move on without looking back.

Mindfulness offers us the opportunity to re-experience this childlike approach. Just like our kids, we can be in the here and now, absorbing everything this moment has to offer.

Obviously, adults can't be like toddlers all the time, nor would we want to be. There isn't anything wrong with problem-solving, analyzing, and being busy. But if that's the only way we know how to be, we can miss the opportunities to smell the flowers, laugh with our kids, connect with our partners or friends, and choose how we want to be in the moment.

PART I

WHERE MINDFULNESS AND PARENTING MEET

CHAPTER 1

MINDFUL PARENTING 101

Sometimes I like to imagine what weekday mornings would be like without any rushing, arguing, or yelling (a mom can dream, right?). Just last week, we went from breakfast to tears in less than three minutes after my husband unwittingly did the pigtails in my daughter's hair too high (inexcusable, I know). She got terribly upset, which led to a meltdown over socks that weren't perfectly positioned beneath her pants. By the time we made it out the front door, my husband was frustrated, my daughter was angry, and we were all running late.

We never wake up thinking, "I'd like to yell at my kid today." Yet despite our best intentions, it can sometimes feel impossible to be a parent and a calm, rational human being at the same time. We want to do our best. But we don't always have the tools to manage everything life throws at us. That's where mindfulness comes in.

What Is Mindfulness?

Mindfulness is a way of training our minds to be in the present moment in a kind, curious, and nonjudgmental manner. Being mindful allows us to be aware of what's actually happening in our minds, bodies, and hearts, rather than getting caught up in our stories, judgments, or worries about what has happened, might happen, or should be happening. We can't always choose or change what's going on, but mindfulness helps us be present so we can choose how we want to relate and respond to our circumstances rather than react on autopilot.

Parenting will always have aspects we can't control. Dinner gets burnt, kids forget their soccer shoes, and traffic is always the worst when we're running late. Six-year-olds will continue to get upset about socks and lose it when their hair isn't perfect.

Without mindfulness, I might have gotten frazzled and joined in the shouting match that began that morning. With mindfulness, I was able to take a moment—and a breath—to see my daughter's and my husband's struggles and proceed with calm support. I stayed grounded and compassionate rather than getting caught up in the storm and possibly making it worse. Mindfulness allowed me to get on with my own work in a focused manner rather than being stressed from the drama of the morning.

That's the beauty of mindfulness—it empowers us, and our kids, to choose how we want to be in any given moment.

Mindfulness is not about sitting still for a long time, and it's definitely not about getting rid of our emotions or stopping all thoughts. Instead, mindfulness is about equipping ourselves with tools so we can be who we already are and do what we're already doing but with more patience, kindness, and focus. We can practice it anywhere at any time for any length of time, regardless of what's going on in and around us.

Imagine the mind like a garden with our habits as seeds. The more we practice kindness, acceptance, and pausing before reacting, the more those seeds will flourish. If we practice impatience, judgment, criticism, and autopilot (consciously or not), we are watering those particular seeds instead. Mindfulness is making a conscious choice about which seeds we plant and which seeds we nourish.

Myths About Mindfulness and Mindful Parenting

I'd like to take a moment to debunk some of the misconceptions about what mindfulness and mindful parenting really are.

MYTH! Mindfulness is about being calm and having no thoughts.

Mindfulness is not about reaching any particular state—calm, blank, or otherwise. Practicing mindfulness is consciously acknowledging the moment as it is. Calmness can be a by-product because we get some space from our immediate reactions and we practice patience and acceptance. If we go into mindfulness expecting total serenity or zero thoughts, we'll usually be disappointed. But if we go in accepting whatever arises and being open to however it feels, we'll be all right regardless of what comes up.

MYTH! Mindfulness means sitting still.

Although we can practice mindfulness in a fixed posture and it can be helpful to practice in quiet, relaxed conditions, we can practice mindfulness anywhere. The goal of mindfulness isn't to sit still but to be present, focused, and kind.

MYTH! Mindfulness takes a lot of time.

Like any habit, the more we practice mindfulness, the more automatic it becomes. Mindfulness can last for a single breath or the time it takes to feel the warmth of the sun on our faces. Mindfulness is repeating short moments of awareness.

MYTH! Mindful parenting makes us doormats.

If mindfulness is all about acceptance, does it mean I have to accept my kid hitting his brother? Of course not! Mindfulness is about being present, so we can choose the appropriate response to any stimulus. As caregivers, we still get to set rules and boundaries and enforce them.

MYTH! Mindful parenting is going to make the whole family happy all the time.

No one is happy all the time. Mindfulness is about being more accepting of all emotions and finding more peace with whatever is going on.

Basic Skills for Mindfulness

Mindfulness is really simple—remembering to practice it is the challenge. You actually already know how to be mindful. Any time you catch yourself relishing your cup of coffee or noticing how quiet the house is after the kids finally settle down, you are being mindful. We can boil mindfulness down to a few basic skills that we'll explore throughout the book.

Noticing the Present Moment: It's all too easy to get caught up in planning, remembering, or worrying (about the past or the future). Mindfulness develops our awareness of what's really happening right now.

Choosing Your Focus: Mindfulness trains us to focus on what we want to focus on when we want to focus on it.

Staying Grounded/Being in Your Body: Our minds take us into worries and plans, but our bodies are always here. Mindful practices focus on grounding the attention to the body and the senses, so we don't get carried away with our thoughts (if we don't want to).

Acknowledging Thoughts and Emotions and Consciously Responding to Them: Thoughts and emotions aren't bad. Our thoughts and feelings only become a problem when we don't know they are happening, when we judge them, or when we get caught up in them. Mindfulness helps us relate differently to our minds and hearts.

Being Curious/Nonjudgmental About This Moment: This aspect of mindfulness is about letting go of how things should be or why this moment isn't good enough and just taking each moment as if it's totally new. Accepting each moment as it is allows us to develop a new way of seeing.

Maintaining a Kind, Compassionate Attitude: Mindfulness encourages us to cultivate an attitude of kindness and friendliness toward ourselves, our loved ones, and everyone else.

Learning mindfulness doesn't have to be stressful or hard. If being mindful becomes another thing on our to-do list, we will either resent it or not do it at all.

You'll notice that this book purposefully focuses on mindful practices for parents before suggesting how they can be shared with kids. Quite simply, we can't help our kids if we aren't present for and kind to ourselves. You just can't pour from an empty cup. We caregivers tend to put our kids first. To really make these practices work for our kids, we first have to turn toward ourselves.

How to Use This Book

The book is divided into eight chapters. Each of the first seven chapters covers an area in which mindfulness may be helpful or needed for adults and kids. Each chapter is organized the same way: (1) introducing a common goal or challenge, (2) discussing how mindfulness can help with that goal or challenge, (3) suggesting activities to cultivate more mindfulness related to the topic, and (4) ending with practice exercises.

Each practice offers self-care tools, parenting support, and suggestions for family participation, including four key elements:

- how adults can apply the practice

- how to apply the practice to parenting

- how to apply the practice in a fun, simple way for families

- how to handle common obstacles that might arise while doing the practice

Each practice can be done anywhere, at any time, and may last from a few seconds to a few minutes.

While each practice is listed in a certain chapter, most can be applied in multiple ways for multiple challenges. The One-Minute Breath Meditation (page 20), for example, does cultivate focus and attention, but it can also be helpful for reducing anxiety, promoting patience, and dealing with difficult emotions. Please see the Practices Index (page 105) at the back of the book to locate specific practices by name.

Practice: Body Scan

Body scans allow us to let go of what's on our minds by connecting with our bodies just as they are right now. Scanning our bodies lets us see where we are holding tension so we can soften those areas if we like. These scans can be done in as little as 3 minutes or as much as 45 minutes.

This activity is simply about feeling what's alive in your body in a kind, curious way without trying to make anything happen or judging what arises.

1. Sit or lie comfortably. Close your eyes if that feels right.
2. Take a moment to notice how you feel.
3. Take a few deep breaths.
4. Allow your breathing to return to normal.
5. Beginning with your feet, focus on any sensations present.
6. You might feel tingling, pressure, warmth, coolness, itching, movement, tension, heaviness, lightness, vibration, or some other sensation. Notice any contact with furniture or clothing. Notice what sensations are present and how they change.

7. Next, bring awareness to the sensations in your legs. Notice temperature, pressure, contact. Notice parts you can feel and parts you can't.

8. Move your attention to your back and buttocks. What can you notice here?

9. Move the awareness to your stomach and chest. Notice if you can feel your breath. Can you feel your heart beating? What else?

10. Tuning into your arms and hands, notice the air touching your skin. Feel any heat or coolness, pressure or lightness. Do the sensations change as you pay attention?

11. Moving to your neck, face, and head, explore each area as if you've never felt them before. What do lips or cheekbones actually feel like? Explore each sensation.

12. When you have finished, notice how you feel now.

13. If you have the time, you might explore each foot individually, then each ankle, calf, knee, and so on.

Applying the Practice

The body scan is a great way to start your day, or you can do it before falling asleep at night. A quick version is perfect when you're stuck in traffic (a nice alternative to getting stressed, and a safer one than getting on the phone) or waiting at the doctor's office. Rather than getting stuck in worries or getting frustrated about waiting, you can remain present and grounded by completing a body scan.

Sharing with Kids

The body scan is lovely to do at bedtime to help let go of the worries or activity of the day. It can be done to relieve anxiety before a test, or you can do a body scan before dinner so everyone is really present at the table. To make the exercise more fun, children might pick a quality that everyone else has to explore, being as creative as they like (for example, where do you feel hottest, mushiest, or most purple in your body?).

Common Obstacles

It's all right if the body scan feels weird or boring. The goal is just to notice whatever is happening. If you feel sleepy, explore how sleepiness feels. If anyone has experienced trauma or is very resistant, a practice with an external focus like the Sense and Savor exercise might feel more comfortable.

Practice: Sense and Savor

This practice asks you to use your senses to explore the present moment, just as it is. Try to be as interested as possible in what's happening, as if the present moment is the very first time you've ever heard a sound or felt a sensation. By paying attention to our senses, we can let go of the busyness of the mind and hone our concentration and ability to be present. This exercise is my favorite practice to do after a long day because it allows me to let go of thinking and connect to and appreciate what's really happening.

1. Start by noticing the feeling of a few deep breaths.
2. Let the breath be natural.
3. Curiously exploring one sense at a time, notice anything and everything you can.
4. What do your eyes see? Notice color, shape, texture, light, darkness, opacity, translucence, shadow. Don't worry about figuring out what you are looking at or what you think of it. Instead, just explore seeing it.
5. Then turn to hearing. What can you hear? See if you can avoid naming the sounds—like "car horn" or "barking dog"—and just notice sounds as they are: loud, quiet, harsh, gentle, soothing, melodious.
6. Continue the exploration with touch (contact, pressure, temperature, vibration, movement), smell (obvious, subtle, powerful, pleasant, unpleasant, familiar, unfamiliar, sour), and taste (bitter, salty, sweet, obvious, subtle, lingering, spicy).
7. Once you've explored each sense, return to your body as a whole and take a few more deep breaths.
8. Notice how you are feeling now—savor this moment of awareness before getting on with your day.

Applying the Practice

Try this practice when you're caught up in worries or when you feel dull or bored. It's a great break if you've been staring at the computer all day. Use this technique as a way to really be present when your kids want to share something with you, even if it's the same dance move or drawing you've seen 900 times before.

Sharing with Kids

This is a sweet exercise for a family walk or time outside in any season. Try it as you brush your child's hair or share a meal. This practice is also nice at bedtime when you can get cozy under the blankets. You could explore taste with local fruits or vegetables. Or you could observe how many different sounds occur just from household objects. Take a moment to marvel at the world around you and the ability of your bodies to explore it.

You might make this exercise a game where family members are blindfolded and have to guess what an object is using only the appropriate sense. You can break up into teams or have the kids find objects for the adults with various textures, tastes, sounds, or scents.

Common Obstacles

To combat the tendency to rush, you might assure yourself that it only takes three extra seconds to savor a bit of
orange rather than immediately reaching for the next
piece. Know that being distracted is all right. With practice,
we can choose to return to the senses when the mind
wanders rather than follow its path.

CHAPTER 2

RECLAIM YOUR FOCUS AND CONCENTRATION

Last week, my daughter and I were reading a bedtime story. During that time, I received two texts, one phone call, and three emails on three different email accounts. It was overwhelming! I wanted to give my daughter (and the story) my full attention, but it seemed like everyone and everything else demanded my complete attention, too.

The Challenge

Most places have laws against distracted driving. What about distracted parenting? Sixty-two percent of kids polled said their parents were too distracted when listening to them. I don't want my relationship with work to take priority over my family, but how do you explain to your boss that you couldn't answer emails because you had to tuck Owlster and Whalie into their own beds before your daughter would go to sleep? With multitasking, text-length communication, the prevalence of ADHD, and our general fear of missing out, distraction feels like a modern epidemic—and it's one that causes us all to miss out.

How Mindfulness Helps

Mindfulness trains us to recognize when our minds wander and empowers us to choose our focus. Being able to make that choice means we can reclaim much of our lives because we are doing what we decide to do, not what's become automatic or routine. With mindfulness, instead of habitually answering emails in our heads while we are reading a story, we can answer emails when we are answering emails and read to our kids when we are reading to our kids. By doing one thing at a time, we actually accomplish more because we are paying attention to what we are doing as it's happening. Everyone in the family thrives with this training because we can focus on our kids and they know they are being heard and seen. And we can be present for our partners and ourselves, too.

Put Mindfulness into Practice

Technology is a fact of our lives. Practicing mindfulness isn't about getting rid of the phone—it's about being able to choose what we pay attention to at any one time. Further, being mindful is about seeing that always reaching for the phone is actually detrimental, not only to our relationships but also to our mental well-being.

It can be helpful to set some limits around technology use. You might try

- making a no-phone rule for the dinner table;

- selecting one evening that is technology-free;

- going for a family walk or outing and leaving the phones behind;

- designating a game night, an arts and crafts after-noon, or a time for activities that can be done without technology.

Here are some suggestions for using technology mindfully:

- Choose specific times to answer emails or attend to texts. Let your kids know: "I want to give you my full attention, but I have to take care of this. Give me 10 minutes, and then I'm all yours."

- Use technology to your advantage with apps that tell you how many times you've checked your phone or how long you've spent on social media. Most people are shocked by the results, and the data can help put things into perspective.

Mindfulness is about choosing which habits we want to build and which ones we want to eliminate. We might not be able to get rid of our phones, but we can loosen their hold on us. The following practices can help build beneficial habits, giving us more say in how we relate to our devices.

Practice: One-Minute Breath Meditation

Breathing practice helps cultivate attention to the present moment, patience, self-awareness, and concentration by giving us one thing to focus on that's happening here and now. Just concentrating on the physical sensations of breathing helps us let go of worries, plans, stresses, and judgments.

Just like the body scan, this breath meditation enables us to be with the sensations of the body in a kind and curious way without needing to make anything happen or stop anything that's already happening. Let your breath be the central focus or anchor of your attention. When the mind wanders, come back to that anchor.

The breath is one of the best mindfulness tools because it's ever present. We can connect to it anytime we wander off into worries, stresses, or plans.

1. Set a timer for at least one minute.
2. Find a posture that feels comfortable, upright, and dignified.
3. Close your eyes or assume a soft gaze in front of you.
4. Take a few deep breaths.
5. Do a quick body scan to notice and let go of any obvious areas of tension.
6. Allow the breath to return to whatever feels normal right now.
7. Just notice what it feels like to breathe naturally.
8. Notice if the breath is smooth, choppy, long, short, deep, shallow, noisy, or tight.
9. When the mind wanders (which it will because that's what minds do), notice where it's gone. Thinking isn't bad or a mistake—it's an opportunity to notice what's happening and to train the mind in a different way.
10. Kindly, gently bring the attention back to the physical sensations of breathing.
11. When the timer goes off, take a moment to notice how you feel. Perhaps even thank yourself for taking this time for self-care.

Applying the Practice

If you need an excellent time-out when things start to get too stressful, do this practice at school drop-off/pick-up or before answering stressful emails. Use it as a pause button before reacting in anger when dishes get dropped or beds still aren't made. Whenever your mind is running away with you, you can turn to your breath.

Sharing with Kids

Try building this technique into your morning routine where everyone takes a breath before heading off to work or school. This breathing meditation is also a great practice before a test or a big game.

It's fun to create different kinds of breaths by moving your body. How would Spider-Man breathe? (Maybe with his arms out like shooting webs?) What about a ballerina, alien, or unicorn? Each family member can create a breath, and then everyone else can guess what it is.

Common Obstacles

If you find you are controlling your breath, that's fine. Just try to let go of getting your breathing right and notice how it feels. If the practice starts to feel boring or repetitive, consider this moment an opportunity to explore something you've never noticed about a thing you've done a million times. Reframing the experience as a chance to learn will help build patience, concentration, and awareness.

Practice: Staying Present for a Boring Task

What parent hasn't heard the dreaded "I'm booooored!" Moreover, what adult hasn't felt bored doing the same task over and over again? We don't really want to do the dishes or take out the garbage. Yet research shows that the more our minds stay on the task at hand, the happier we actually are. The more we can choose how we relate to any event, the more we train our minds to be where and how we want them to be.

The mindful approach to boredom is to see that our perception of what is boring is not a fact but a judgment of the mind. The antidote is to seek out something interesting by paying attention to what's happening as if you've never experienced it before.

Just like we can't get rid of our phones, we can't stop taking out the garbage or doing the laundry. If we dismiss these tasks as a waste of time, we are actually dismissing much of what happens in our lives. But if we use these times as a chance to connect with our senses, our kids, and ourselves, we can see that there's something to appreciate in every moment, even in the chore-filled ones.

1. Set the intention to notice what's happening without judging it or trying to change it. This exercise is about being present and letting go of any need to make this moment anything other than what it is right now.
2. Take a few deep breaths. Notice how your body and mind feel.

3. Allow the breath to return to normal.
4. Turn your attention to the task at hand. Rather than letting preconceived judgments dictate how you feel, try to anchor your attention to your senses. If driving, notice how the steering wheel feels under your fingertips. Notice the rumble of the car beneath your body or the sound of the wind. If you're washing the dishes, feel the warmth of the water and the foamy soap on your skin. Notice the feeling of the plate or the sound of clinking glasses.
5. Ask yourself, "What can I be interested in right now? What are my senses telling me?"
6. You can notice how many stories or thoughts your mind has about the present moment ("too boring," "more important things to do," "partner should be doing this instead"). You can be curious about these too, and then bring the attention back to the senses.

Applying the Practice

The key to attention isn't forcing your mind to be glued to only one thing. It's recognizing that your mind will wander and that you can bring it back by finding something—anything—that you can be interested in at that moment. This ability can be so helpful for those parenting moments that you've done a million times, like helping your kids brush their teeth or pick up their toys.

Sharing with Kids

Mary Poppins said, "In every job that must be done, there is an element of fun." Mindfulness taps into that fun by connecting to what's interesting about this moment. When kids moan, "This is boring," try to help them find a way to see it from a new angle. Instead of just cleaning, what if you are aliens doing this job for the first time? Or what if you are the interstellar scientists describing these basic human tasks to a being from outer space? For older kids, have them notice how the task feels to their senses, rather than focusing on the story in their minds.

Common Obstacles

Chances are you will hear "This is dumb" from either your own brain or your kids' mouths. That's okay. See if you can frame it as just one possibility instead of the singular truth. Sure, it might feel dumb, but that judgment doesn't actually help anyone—it just makes the task even more unpleasant. By asking how you could turn the chore into a game, you can get the job done and find more enjoyment in the moment as well.

Practice: Mindful Eating

Mindful eating is another way to practice paying attention to what's happening in our bodies and our senses without rushing through it or getting too caught up in judgment. This practice builds awareness and concentration because we so rarely just eat while we are eating.

1. Choose a food to eat mindfully. It can be one bite or an entire meal.
2. Set the intention to focus entirely on eating. For this practice, set aside conversation and reading material and turn off any devices or music.
3. Employ all of your senses, one at a time.

   Sight: Take the time to see all the colors of the food. Notice how the light hits the food and any textures, shapes, symmetry, or contours.

   Sound: Although your food itself might not make noise, you can listen to the sound of chewing, swallowing, lifting the fork, and setting it down.

   Smell: Before you begin eating, take the time to breathe and smell the food. Notice if the smell is sharp or dull, sweet or bitter. Observe how quick the mind is to categorize smell based on memory.

Touch: Notice how your body feels sitting in the chair. Pay attention to the sensation of the fork or spoon in your hand. Notice how the food feels in your mouth. Let it linger on your tongue even before you take a bite. What do chewing and swallowing feel like?

Taste: The last step is actually tasting the food. Go slowly, one bite at a time. Put your fork down between bites. Really let the taste linger. Take a breath before going for the next bite.

Applying the Practice

Try to truly focus on your morning coffee or a bite of a bagel. Let meals take longer than they might otherwise and do your best to really enjoy the food—and the company. Eating mindfully benefits families because it means you are focusing on the moment, choosing to spend time together rather than rushing off to do something else, and it trains patience because you're challenging your usual habits.

Sharing with Kids

Who wouldn't enjoy spending more time eating dessert? What does that very first lick of an ice-cream cone taste like? Have you ever really paid attention to the texture of broccoli?

Use this exercise as an opportunity to connect with the family by discovering foods you've never tried before and guessing what they might taste like (dragon fruit or other less familiar fruits work well, even for picky eaters).

Common Obstacles

Time is the big challenge here. Pick this practice when you don't have to rush off to ballet class or robotics camp (though you can savor and notice just one bite, even if it takes place in the car before practice). If family meals are the only time to connect, you might designate just the first bite or the last two minutes to practice mindful eating so you can catch up for the rest of the meal.

MINDFUL THINKING

Do you ever feel like your mind has a mind of its own? That when you're trying to prepare dinner or listen to your children's stories, you drift into daydreams, judgments, and worries? *Does this food have too many chemicals? What if he talks too much at school? If the economy keeps getting worse, what will we do? I have so much work right now. I feel so old. Why am I the only one who takes care of this? Other parents can handle this stuff better than I can. I wonder what's on TV?* Although estimates vary, we can assume that we have approximately 50,000 thoughts per day. It's no wonder our minds can't stay focused on just one thing!

One of the most persistent myths about mindfulness is that you're only doing it right when you stop thinking entirely. Not only is that assumption untrue, it's virtually impossible. Mindfulness isn't about getting rid of thoughts—it isn't about getting rid of anything. Mindfulness is just about seeing what's alive in this moment, exploring it with compassionate attention, and then choosing whether we want to continue considering what we've noticed after we've acknowledged it mindfully. Being mindful of our thoughts means that we're not preoccupied—we're aware that we're thinking. Mindfulness enables us to see when thinking is helpful and when the mind is just in its own spin cycle.

Thinking only becomes a problem when we get so caught up in it that we lose sight of what's happening right now. We either miss the present moment because we're stuck in memories, plans, worries, or daydreams, or we can't accept the present moment because we're trapped in judgment, anxiety, comparisons, and expectations of how things should be different. Thinking happens. Our task is to be responsible for how we act on it.

Here, "be responsible" means to be able to respond. That's what we want to do with our thinking and the rest of our experiences: respond mindfully in a way that promotes our well-being and our focus on the present moment. Research shows that mindfulness helps practitioners gain some perspective on and distance from endless thinking or rumination, which leads to less self-referential thinking, less mind wandering, and less of a feeling that the mind has a mind of its own.

So how do you actually practice mindfulness?

One way to practice mindfulness of thinking is to just watch the thoughts come and go. Rather than getting caught up in the content of the thought, see if you can simply observe your own thinking mind. Watching your mind work is like sitting on a bridge and watching cars go by—you just notice the thoughts (how many, how fast, different colors). Whenever you notice you've been caught up in one of those thoughts, pause to see it, acknowledge where your mind has gone, and then gently, without recrimination, come back to what's happening right now: this body, this breath, these thoughts coming and going.

That sounds great, but what do you do if your thoughts seem inescapable?

Sometimes, we get stuck on a particular thought. Instead of trying to get rid of the thought, hating it, analyzing it, or judging ourselves for it, explore what's happening in this moment of feeling stuck by doing a quick meditation like the One-Minute Breath Meditation (page 20).

Take a few deep breaths. Feel your feet on the floor. Acknowledge what it's like to feel stuck in the thought. Let go of the content of the thought, and notice what's happening in your body. Notice any areas of tightness, tension, heat, or tingling. Chances are, deep emotions are associated with the thought. Kindly explore them and where you feel them in your body. As gently as possible, try to sit with these emotions and sensations, without needing to make anything happen. Notice how strong or weak the thoughts are. If you get caught in the story of the thought or feel overwhelmed, come back to the feeling of sitting and breathing. Notice how the thoughts and feelings change as you observe them.

As you explore the moment, you can see that this thought, however powerful, is just a thought. It's not a fact. You don't have to believe it right now (even if it comes back again and again). You can even ask, "Is this thought actually helping me in this moment?" The purpose of this question isn't to analyze the content of the thought but to ask about the nature of the thought and to recognize your ability to decide your relationship to the thought. If you can see that the thought isn't helpful, you can choose to repeatedly turn your attention back to your body and breath.

Although turning your attention away from a thought isn't easy, it can be extremely empowering. You see that you have more say over your thoughts than they have over you.

What you might find is that thoughts act like kindling for emotions, particularly painful ones. Your kid draws on the walls with permanent marker, and you lose your temper. After you settle down, you feel relatively okay . . . until that thought comes back up. *How could he do this? I told him not to play with those markers! What if he never gets better at listening? Am I just a bad parent?* And then you feel the anger all over again. Awareness of your body and your breathing acts as an antidote. No, mindfulness won't clean the walls, and it won't make your children better at listening. But being mindful will allow you to be gentle with yourself, your mind, and your children when you most need to.

For most parents, worries and fears are part of the job. Our minds run away with us, but mindfulness lets us choose which thoughts we want to listen to, and it allows us to see which thoughts are helping us and which ones are just causing trouble. We get to be responsible for what we think. Some thoughts are very much like those kids on the playground or in detention that you don't want your child associating with—bullies. The good news is that, like bullies, these thoughts thrive on attention. If we call these thoughts what they are ("There's another nasty thought some part of my brain thinks I should believe") and consciously choose kindness and attention to our bodies and senses, those bullying thoughts lose their power.

Just like footprints in the sand, the hormonal outbursts of a teenager, or the attention of a toddler, thoughts can come and go if we let them.

PART II

BECOMING EMOTIONALLY MINDFUL

CHAPTER 3

GRATITUDE AND JOY

The other day, we stumbled upon my daughter's old onesies. She couldn't stop giggling as she attempted to put them on, remarking about how tiny they were. Swaddling and peek-a-boo felt like yesterday. One almost universal truth about parenting is that while the days can feel interminably long, the years pass by in a flash. Haven't we all had conversations with other caregivers about how we just wish they didn't grow up so fast? Sometimes I just want to hold on to a moment and make it last forever.

Obviously, we can't stop time. And we wouldn't want to stop our children from growing and changing, even if those changes challenge us as parents. But we can choose how we connect to those moments. Instead of grasping on to those moments, we can be present for them, enjoying them as they happen, and appreciating them to their fullest. Rather than regretting the passing of those sweet times, we can use mindfulness to cultivate gratitude and joy.

This aspect of mindfulness isn't about being overly optimistic or naïve, nor is the goal to ignore reality or deny hardship. Gratitude and joy aren't built-in traits that you either have or don't. Gratitude and joy are actually qualities that we can choose to cultivate, like muscles that grow if we exercise them in the right way. Being grateful not only improves physical and mental health, but also the more we practice gratitude, the more readily available it is and the more joy we experience in our lives.

The neuroscience community describes this ability to retrain our minds as experience-dependent neuroplasticity. It's a fancy term for something pretty remarkable: Our brains get good at what they practice, and we can use the mind to change the physical structures of the brain. In an article for *Scientific American*, journalist Tom Ireland lays out the multitude of ways that paying attention mindfully actually shrinks the part of our brains that acts as an alarm bell and starts the stress response (the amygdala) and grows the part that's responsible for emotional regulation and decision-making (the prefrontal cortex). In other words, you *can* teach an old dog (or parent) new tricks. If our mind is like a garden, then we have to ask ourselves what seeds we really want to be nurturing—what kind of person and parent do we want to be? Almost all of us would choose to practice more joy, kindness, and gratitude. Mindfulness gives us the tools to do just that. And the more we practice, the better we get.

Put Gratitude and Joy into Practice

The basic idea here is to seek out, notice, and appreciate more of the things that give us simple pleasures and make us feel good. We don't need to ignore the negative or bad, but we can choose to focus on the good and cultivate more joy and gratitude in our lives. Just looking for something to appreciate helps to change your brain, so focus on wholesome (healthy) pleasures. That's not to say you can't enjoy a glass of wine or your favorite movie—just notice that the pleasure isn't so much about the alcohol or the distraction but about letting yourself feel good in any given moment.

Practice: Right Now, I'm Grateful For . . .

This practice is deceptively simple but incredibly powerful. It's just about taking the time to notice and focus on things that you appreciate.

1. Start by taking a few deep breaths, which encourages you to let go of the past or future and come back to the here and now.
2. Consider three things for which you are grateful. These can be something big, like an upcoming vacation, or very small, like a moment of quiet or a soft blanket.
3. Let yourself linger on these appreciations. Notice how being grateful feels in your body.

4. While you can simply consider these by yourself, a more habit-building, joy-inducing practice is to write down what you are grateful for and share your list or read it aloud to a friend, partner, or loved one.

5. When your partner shares or reads their gratitude list, take a breath or two and truly give them your attention. If your mind wanders off, just notice that your attention has drifted and bring it back to the present moment and your intention to be grateful. Notice how someone else's gratitude makes you feel in your body, and explore what it's like to be truly happy for someone else.

Applying the Practice

The more you do this practice, the more habitual it becomes, so try to make it a regular part of a morning or bedtime routine: brush your teeth, wash your face, and practice gratitude. Letting go of what happened earlier or what might take place tomorrow is a sweet way to start and end the day.

If you find yourself anxious or upset, one of the most effective remedies is to turn toward gratitude. Being thankful might be the last thing you want to do if your kid is out past curfew and isn't answering your texts. But gratitude can actually calm the mind and bring you back to the present moment, so you don't get even more stressed by worry.

Sharing with Kids

It's helpful to make this a regular family habit and have everyone share their gratitude over the dinner table or at bedtime. You can share something you are grateful for generally and then be more specific. You can also say what you appreciate about each other, which helps build gratitude and interpersonal connection. With little kids, you can ask, "What made you happy today?"

Another great option is to create gratitude jars with your kids. Decorate mason jars or old jam jars any way you like (glitter glue, ribbon, stickers, markers, colored paper). Then cut out small strips of paper and write three things you each are grateful for to keep in the jar. Store the jars somewhere where you will see them regularly to remind yourself not only to keep exploring your gratitude but also that you are grateful for so many things, you need a jar to hold them all. Younger kids can draw their subjects of gratitude if they can't write them.

Common Obstacles

What if you just don't feel grateful right now? It happens. While you could still look for even the tiniest thing (indoor plumbing?), you can also give yourself a break, recognize that this is a particularly tough moment, and that it's okay. This difficult moment is a lovely opportunity to go back and read old items of gratitude and see that this, too, will pass.

Practice: Enjoying the Good

Like Sense and Savor (page 12), Enjoying the Good is about focusing on the sensory experience of the present moment with as much interest and curiosity as possible. The bonus is that you get to linger on something that feels particularly good and make that feeling last for a while.

1. This exercise can be done spontaneously when you feel good, or it can be explored in a time set aside specifically for this purpose.
2. As always, take a few deep breaths. Let go of anything in your mind that you don't need right now. The groceries and the school forms can wait for just these few moments.
3. Find something good in the moment or in your memory. As you eat a piece of chocolate, feel the sun on your face, or notice yourself laughing with your children, take the time to really pay attention to what it feels like. Pause and delight in this good thing.
4. Notice each sense as much as you can. Really linger on each feeling, magnifying it as much as you would if something were going wrong.
5. Imagine absorbing this feeling into your body and making it a permanent part of you.
6. Before you move on with the rest of your day, take an extra breath and soak in the moment one more time.

Applying the Practice

So often we dismiss a compliment that someone gives us, or we take a quick picture of a sunset and rush inside to put the kids to bed. This practice is about really staying with those moments when they happen. As you start to do this, you'll notice more and more small moments throughout your parenting day that bring you gratitude and joy. It then becomes easier to move past the times when the kids are bickering or your four-year-old decides to dump an entire container of yogurt on his head.

Sharing with Kids

See how long you can make a piece of chocolate last. Or find all of the different ways you can laugh. Who can make the silliest face? This is all about connecting to anything that encourages the feelings of joy in the moment.

Common Obstacles

The biggest issue here is just remembering to enjoy the good. Making this practice part of your daily routine is helpful. Kids tend to master this technique more quickly than adults, so they can be empowered to remind us to stop and smell the roses—and enjoy the chocolate.

Practice: Move Your Body

If you've ever noticed that you feel a bit happier after you exercise, it's not just you. Physical activity has been proven to reduce stress, help sleep, and improve mood, self-esteem, and cognitive function. Generally, the more we move, the better we tend to feel.

1. The idea here is to move your body in a way that is comfortable and feels good.
2. You might try gently swaying from side to side, swinging your arms back and forth, doing some light stretches, dancing, going for a walk, or even giving yourself a gentle massage.
3. Let your body tell you what would feel good rather than trying to think about it or get it "right."
4. Sometimes just reaching down and stretching out your back or rolling your shoulders is enough.
5. Take a moment to notice how your body feels and to appreciate this opportunity to move.

Applying the Practice

Use this technique when you need a break (whether at work or at home). When emotions start to get too big or you begin to feel overwhelmed, pause and move your body, even if you only walk to the next room. Movement helps calm emotions and lets us self-regulate. It can actually bring an over- or under-aroused nervous system that's in fight-flight-freeze mode back online. If helping the kids with their homework is getting too tricky or everyone is arguing, take a quick walk around the block or even just to the living room.

Sharing with Kids

Physical exercise is a wonderful way for kids to break up a stressful school project or to change a grumpy mood. For the whole family, try a one-minute dance party. Take turns picking the music or just dance in the car to whatever is on the radio. Play red rover, hide-and-seek, or tag. Have races as a family, making them as silly as possible (who can crab walk or slither across the floor the fastest?). Active play increases endorphins, which make us all feel good.

Common Obstacles

It can be very hard to do the thing we need most in any given moment, especially if what we need involves breaking the momentum of a bad mood (like getting up and moving instead of stewing). It can be helpful to remind yourself that, even when it feels impossible, you still have the choice in how you respond and how the rest of a conversation or day might go.

CHAPTER 4

DEALING WITH ANXIETY AND STRESS

Last fall, my daughter broke her arm when she fell off the monkey bars. Once the shock wore off and the pain subsided, she was totally fine. I, however, was a wreck. When she had her cast on, I was terrified she would bang it. And when she got it off and returned to those monkey bars, my heart was in my throat. Using my mindfulness tools, I was able to see that my worries were getting the best of me and that I could come back to the present moment where everything was actually okay. But my default was definitely full-on anxious-parent mode.

I'm one of those people who assumes I need to call the hospital if my family is 10 minutes late coming home. If they gave awards for stress, my trophy case would be full. I remember panicking while pregnant with my daughter:

How could I possibly take care of someone else when I can barely handle myself?

Now, stress isn't all bad. We actually need some stress to push us to work hard, accomplish goals—even have kids in the first place. Good stress builds resilience, but stress becomes a problem when the demands of our lives consistently overwhelm our ability to meet those demands.

When we perceive a threat, our brains trigger a hormonal and physiological response: fight-flight-freeze mode. This response evolved to help us survive in life-threatening situations. Once the threat passes, the nervous system is supposed to return to a deactivated state. The problem for many of us is that our nervous systems can't tell the difference between a life-threatening situation and our concern that our children are eating too much (or too little). So little things are actually over-activating us—that is, small issues are stressing us out because we feel we cannot meet those demands. If we are always feeling threatened, the nervous system never gets to relax, leading to mental and physical imbalance and dysfunction.

As parents and caregivers, we know that demands and stresses are part of the package. It's not like we're going to stop worrying any time soon, so we need to respond to stress in a healthier way. With mindfulness, we can see when we get caught up in fears and thoughts and then choose how much power to give them. We get the tools to deactivate a triggered nervous system and find more balance in our minds and our lives.

Practice: Check Your Own Nervous System First

As I raced to school after my daughter broke her arm, I was scared and anxious. But when I arrived, despite hearing her sobs echo through the hallways, I made myself pause, take several deep breaths, and walk calmly (albeit quickly) to her. I had to get my fear under control before I could support her. If I had rushed in, yelling at teachers, screaming about how horrible this is, she would have panicked. The key to supporting anyone experiencing any sort of trauma is to check your own nervous system first. Kids regulate their nervous systems to the grown-ups in their lives. My daughter needed me to bring her to my level of calm rather than me joining and contributing to her state of panic.

When a car cuts you off or you read bad news or you're in a heightened state for whatever reason, try this exercise.

1. You'll likely have very loud thoughts running through your mind, and you'll feel powerful sensations in your body (heat, flushed cheeks, heart pounding). As you notice what's happening, take a few deeper breaths and acknowledge this moment as it is right now.
2. Whatever you feel in this moment is fine—you don't have to get rid of it. You don't have to like your emotion, but you can choose to accept it, just as it is.

3. Once you see your immediate reaction, you can choose how to proceed mindfully. Remind yourself that you're in control, even if your mind and body are doing their own things.
4. Take a few more deep breaths. Use your senses to bring you back to the here and now.
5. Feel your feet on the floor or your bum in the chair. Notice what you see, hear, smell, or taste. Remind yourself that you're choosing to slow down.
6. It can be helpful to focus on two senses at the same time. Can you feel your feet and listen to the sounds in the room?
7. As you finish the practice, take a moment to notice how you're feeling. If you still feel very activated, that's okay. You can repeat the exercise if you need to.
8. Take a moment to thank yourself for making a more supportive choice in a difficult situation.

Applying the Practice

Any phone call from school, news from the doctor, or challenging email can be an opportunity to apply this technique. When your children are panicking about their own bad news, see if you can check your own nervous system first. You can even do this with colleagues or other family members. Just like we feed off each other's stress, we can find balance from someone else's stability.

Sharing with Kids

Help kids take a breath before they panic. You might even overexaggerate your deep breathing to show them what you're doing. Try having them count backward from 10, taking a breath with each number. Know that you are giving them a gift by doing this and teaching them that self-care isn't selfish.

Common Obstacles

I hear you: "You want me to be calm when my kid is in the hospital? Are you crazy?" I'm not saying it's easy. And I'm also not saying that your heart won't still be racing or tears won't be ready to flow. It's not about denying how you feel but choosing what will best support you and your children at that moment.

Practice: 5-4-3-2-1 Grounding

When we get overwhelmed or anxious, the mind goes into overdrive. It doesn't matter that I know I'm being ridiculous—my brain just can't stop picturing worst-case scenarios, and my body can't stop freaking out. In times like these, telling ourselves to calm down doesn't help. We need to give ourselves something to do to come back to this moment and to know that we are safe and everything is, or will be, okay.

1. Breathe. If you need this practice, it's likely you feel overwhelmed and your breath is probably fast and shallow. A deep breath is actually a cue to the nervous system that you are safe.
2. As much as you can, let go of the mind's commentary and come back to what your body feels right now.
3. Look around for five things that you see (tree, pencil, blue sky). It helps to say these things out loud.
4. Then focus on four things you can feel (air, clothing, floor under your feet, cold hands).
5. Next pay attention to three things that you hear (car, stomach rumbling, breathing, air conditioner).
6. Notice two things that you smell (or recall two smells that you enjoy).
7. Explore one thing that you taste (any lingering taste in your mouth).
8. Don't worry about getting it right. The idea is to just give the brain something to do that anchors it to this time and place.
9. Once you're done, take another deep breath. Notice how you feel now.

Applying the Practice

Use this when everything feels like too much, whether you're at work, with your children, or just in your own mind. It's a built-in time-out. It's helpful to practice this when you aren't anxious so you have the tool readily available when you need it. If your kids are yelling, the phone is ringing, and you start to lose it, take the time to ground yourself before responding. You can also use this when you feel spaced out or disconnected and want to be present for your children.

Sharing with Kids

Modeling the grounding practice will normalize this behavior for your kids so share your responses out loud to demonstrate your self-regulation habits. Help kids combine this with the Sense and Savor practice (page 12) so everyone starts to notice their senses more in moments of ease and moments of stress. It's a great method when tensions are just starting to escalate. A shorter version works with kids of any age when they are getting upset. Asking them (gently or playfully) to connect to their senses breaks the momentum of a meltdown, helping them calm down.

In order to make this habitual, play around with it regularly. On car trips, ask everyone how many sounds they can hear or who can feel the most different textures without moving.

Common Obstacles

As with most of these practices, the biggest obstacle is remembering to do it in those activated moments. That's why engaging in this exercise regularly can really make a difference.

Practice: Seeing the Whole Picture

Anxiety is relentless worrying about nothing and everything. It's your analytical mind trying to help solve problems. Believe it or not, worrying activates the brain's reward centers because it gives your mind something to do. But all that activity actually fuels stress, and we know that just telling ourselves to stop worrying doesn't work. So in this exercise, rather than ignoring what's happening or feeling bad about being stressed, we give our brains something more helpful to focus on.

1. Focus on an object—anything that you can see or even bring to mind.
2. Take several moments to really see and explore the object. Notice all of its colors, textures, and shapes. Imagine you were asked to draw the object or write a poem about it.
3. Then consider how the object got here. What are all the steps it went through to get to this moment—think about the people and resources involved. (If you are looking at a cereal box, for example, you might consider where the grains came from, that the grains needed sunlight and rain to grow, that the packaging came from trees, that the trees needed to be processed, someone was needed to do the processing, and on and on.)

4. Take a moment to recognize that you are part of that connection and explore all of the things that brought you to this moment right now.
5. Gratitude is actually one of the best ways to counter anxiety and stress (see chapter 3). As you do this exercise, you can take a moment to feel truly grateful for this object and all the amazing connections it brings to light.

Applying the Practice

Use this exercise anytime you feel like your mind has a mind of its own. If you feel down or blue, stressed, anxious, or even bored, take a moment to explore this technique. When you are having a particularly difficult time with your kid(s), see if you can pause and connect to this being that you have nurtured. Think of how far you've come and how you got to this moment.

Sharing with Kids

This practice is a lovely way to cultivate respect for our world and the people in it. Before the family eats, you might reflect on the incredible trip the food took to make its way to your plate. If you buy new clothes or get a book, you can marvel at what's actually in your hands—not just an object, but a relationship to the whole world.

Common Obstacles

This exercise might feel silly to you or your kids. Silly is great—it makes us feel lighter and allows us to let go of our anxiety, even for a moment. Don't worry about getting this technique right or trying to feel a certain way. Just notice whatever arises.

CHAPTER 5

MANAGING ANGER AND DIFFICULT EMOTIONS

It seemed like the unsolicited advice started pouring in the moment I announced my pregnancy. I got everything from "Sleep when the baby sleeps" to "Don't eat sushi" to "Don't let her take out student loans when she's in college." Thanks, everyone.

Through it all, there was one piece of advice that really stuck: Call everything a phase. Baby isn't sleeping? Just a phase. Kid throws tantrums every day at 4 p.m.? Phase. Teenager only speaks in grunts? Phase. Doesn't matter what the phase is or why it's happening—teething, a growth spurt, or Saturn going retrograde—the point is it won't last forever. If the problem is just a phase, then it has an ending and we can get through it.

This advice helped immensely when my daughter got sick when she was 11 months old. She was barely eating or sleeping—totally miserable. My husband and I felt awful and at a loss as to how to make her comfortable. My panic was intense, and I felt overwhelmed with fear. It felt like she would never be healthy and none of us would ever sleep well again.

And then she got better. Everything went back to normal. Until the next time something came up. And the time after that. My habit is to assume the worst, and I get overwhelmed with fear that feels like it will last forever. My mindfulness practice lets me see that my fear, too, is just a phase.

Our emotions and moods are actually very much like these phases our kids go through. Just like we don't ask for and can't control growth spurts, teething, puberty, or tantrums, we don't always ask for and usually can't control our emotions and moods or those of our children. But with mindfulness, we can remember to notice these emotions, know they won't last, and be kind as we experience a tantrum or meltdown (theirs or ours).

In fact, difficult emotions are really only difficult because we've decided we don't like them. We actually make it harder on ourselves because we don't want to feel this feeling just as it is. There's an overwhelming sense that this moment shouldn't be like this. It's natural that we prefer some emotions more than others, just like we are bound to like some of our children's phases more than others. But none of our emotions are inherently bad. Some are just more challenging or further from what we expected in that moment.

Practice: Name That Emotion

We can make emotions less overwhelming simply by naming them. By identifying and acknowledging our emotions, we can reduce their power over us.

1. Wherever you are, find even the smallest opportunity to pause and take a breath or two.
2. Notice what's happening in your body and mind without needing to change anything or blame yourself or anyone else for it.
3. Feel your feet on the floor. Notice every part of you that's in contact with something else.
4. Gently inquire: "What am I feeling right now?"
5. You can name any emotion or combination of emotions or just consider any word or sound that remotely represents your current state.
6. Once you have even a tiny sense of the emotion you're experiencing, see if you can be curious about how it feels in your body.
7. Explore how those sensations change. Notice how easy it is to get caught up in thoughts of the trigger or the consequences, and then come back to your physical experience and the label itself.
8. This exercise isn't about figuring out or analyzing why you feel this way—it's just about noticing, feeling, and caring for this moment as it is.

Applying the Practice

You can do this exercise on the fly or during a time set aside for reflection.

This is one of those "the more you do it, the more you'll keep doing it" practices. In the heat of an argument with your children, see if you can pause, check out what's happening in your mind and body, and name the emotions. That pause can make all the difference between fueling the fight and being able to gain some perspective. Try to incorporate this technique throughout your day with different moods and emotions, not just when things are challenging.

Sharing with Kids

We know that kids model our behavior, so the more we gently acknowledge our moods and emotions, the more they will, too. They can see that it's okay to feel however they feel and that they don't have to react when emotions are really powerful. It's also helpful to be vocal about your emotions. You can tell your kids, "I'm feeling sad right now" or "I'm so happy to see you, and I also had a really rough day. How about if I lie down for five minutes, and then we can play?" That communication not only normalizes those feelings and builds emotional vocabulary, it also lets your kids see that they don't have to take your moods or emotions personally.

With little kids, have them name, draw, or act out their emotions. You might even make a habit of asking the family, "What are you feeling right now?"

Common Obstacles

I get it—no one likes feeling bad. Yet this exercise isn't about making you feel bad but rather about acknowledging the feeling that's already there and then choosing how you want to relate to it. If you hate the emotion, then you'll just feel bad about feeling bad. If you ignore the feeling, it usually comes back stronger than ever.

If you ever start to feel overwhelmed, open your eyes (if they are closed) and come back to the feeling of your feet on the ground or the experience of your senses.

Practice: Taking Care of Feelings with a Mindful SNACK

Are you one of those caregivers who always has a snack in your bag, car, purse, and office, just in case the kids get hungry and cranky? Have you ever rummaged through your bag to find your wallet and out tumble three granola bars and two juice boxes? We know those snacks come in handy when our kids need sustenance. This practice is all about giving ourselves a little bit of nourishment, too: a snack of mindfulness.

Use the SNACK acronym to notice and take care of and nourish your current emotions, whatever they are.

Stop: Pause, take a moment, and breathe.

Notice/Name: Explore what's happening right now and give it a name. You might inquire: What's alive in my mind and body? What emotions are present right now? What do the emotions feel like? Where do I feel them? This exercise builds on Name That Emotion (page 59) and the Body Scan (page 10).

Allow/Acknowledge/Accept: You don't have to change anything that's happening. Just see that it's happening and that it's okay. You can accept the situation, your thoughts and feelings, and yourself just as they are.

Care/Compassion: Take care of your feelings. Instead of hating your emotions or trying to get rid of them, what would it be like to truly care for them? Imagine actually holding that fear or that anger the way you'd hold your children if they had a bad dream.

Kindness/Knowing: Instead of thinking, "I'm just an angry person" or "There's something wrong with me," try thinking, "This emotion is here right now, and it's okay." Kindness allows us to let go of judgments and the need to make this feeling go away. Knowing is seeing that this emotion won't last forever and that it doesn't define you.

Applying the Practice

Like the Name That Emotion practice on page 59, this technique should be used when things feel fine in order to practice for when things aren't so great. Notice the sweet moments with your kids, as well as the rougher ones. Start to pay attention to which emotions are connected to certain actions and behaviors and use that understanding to communicate with your family about your needs and theirs. However you feel, see if you can let your emotions come and go, being curious about them without getting caught up in the story behind them.

Sharing with Kids

When exploring this exercise with smaller children, ask them to describe their feelings using colors, shapes, or animals. Let them give the emotion a name. Have them draw a picture of Crabby, the grumpy crab. Or ask them how Gus, the sad walrus would walk. What face would a scaredy-cat make?

Regardless of your child's age, the point is to encourage kind, curious exploration of all feelings, to promote the idea that all feelings are always valid. Even if we don't like our emotions, we don't have to beat ourselves up about them. We can see that feelings don't last and that they don't define us—they are just visiting for a little bit.

Common Obstacles

Sometimes you just can't tell what you feel. That's fine. Mindfulness is not about getting the right answer—it's about noticing.

If your emotions are ever overwhelming, take another deep breath, open your eyes if they're closed, and connect to your senses. Remind yourself that you are safe and that this is just another phase.

Practice: All the Space in This Place

Becoming a parent is a dramatic event, no matter how it happens. For me, there was one surprising aspect of being in labor that's stuck with me through the years. I learned that no matter how intense the contractions are, the body gets a break between them—a state of rest. But if the mind is panicking about the next contraction, or is still stuck on the last one, you don't get that much-needed rest.

This exercise is all about noticing the spaces in between the emotional activity. Big emotions often feel like they are constant and will last forever. But if we can look a bit closer, we can see that there are actually spaces to rest.

1. Although this technique can be done as a formal activity, it works better if you start to get curious about what's actually involved in emotions and what they feel like as they are happening.

2. Explore how the emotion feels in your body. Notice how often it changes, even subtly. It shifts and gets stronger and weaker.

3. Notice the spaces in between your emotions. No matter how angry, sad, or frustrated you are, there is always a space in there where you don't feel that emotion or you focus on something else. Notice that even in the worst moods, you still get a few breaks.

4. See if you can rest in those breaks. Take a breath and notice when the emotion feels less powerful.

5. It's important to remember that this practice is not about denying the feeling or trying to make it go away. Nor is this exercise about figuring out why you feel this way. The goal is to just be with the emotion as it is and look for places to rest.

Applying the Practice

This exercise is helpful for changing how we relate to our moods. When you feel like you're stuck in anger or over-whelmed with frustration, it helps to see that those moods and emotions aren't constant. Then you can choose which parts to focus on and identify with.

Parenting has so many ups and downs and everything in between. This technique encourages us to look for the breaks, not just the chaos. Focusing on the spaces in between emotions is also helpful for when we get into a negative pattern, perhaps even calling ourselves bad parents. We aren't bad—we're just having a rough time right now.

Sharing with Kids

Kids of any age feel overwhelmed by their feelings, too. Encourage them to notice what the emotion does, how it changes, moves, and shifts. You might ask: "What do you feel in your body right now? Where did the sadness go?"

Common Obstacles

It's difficult to step back and observe the emotion rather than get caught up in it. That's where consistent practice can be so helpful. The more you practice observing your emotions, the more you can see that they change and shift and that you can find space between them and from them.

PART III

BECOMING A MINDFUL CITIZEN

CHAPTER 6

PROMOTING PATIENCE AND COMPASSION

My daughter and I say the same phrase whenever we are in the car and we hear a siren: "I hope everyone is okay." It's a simple way to connect to other people, offer our compassion for someone who might be in pain, and practice patience by seeing that any inconvenience we might experience (by missing a light, for example) is secondary to someone else's needs at that time. It's an example of mindfulness in action—a moment to stop our usual way of being, notice what's happening, and choose a compassionate response.

Mindfulness isn't about being good at sitting still in a dark room or being able to pay attention when everything is quiet and calm. We practice in ideal conditions so that we can be patient and compassionate when challenges arise in the real world. Most of us start to practice mindfulness because we are frustrated or dissatisfied with our usual way of doing things and how we habitually relate to others and ourselves. We know there's got to be a better way.

Mindfulness doesn't dictate what the way forward is. Instead, it enables us to use the power of our minds to create our realities. What we believe, focus on, or practice, we make real. If something happens and we see it as a problem, it becomes one. If we continually yell at our kids or beat ourselves up for making mistakes, that habit becomes the way things are.

But if we can learn to see each moment as an opportunity to cultivate the qualities we want more of in our lives, then we can learn and grow from everything, even the two-year-old putting rocks up his nose or the 14-year-old who declares she's a vegetarian except for pepperoni pizza (with apologies to my own parents—it was a phase).

As parents, we want to nurture our children. We want to help them as much as possible and give them the best tools to survive and thrive in a world that is often harsh and challenging. One of the best ways to support them is to nurture those qualities in them, and us, that will enable us all to help ourselves and each other in the world.

Practice: Just Like Me

The goal of this practice is to shift how we relate to people who we find difficult or strange. Instead of seeing every-thing that separates us, we can see how similar we actually are, thus building compassion and empathy. Practicing compassion can increase happiness and self-esteem.

1. Take a few breaths. (I keep repeating this because it's the best cue to your system that something different is about to happen.)
2. Let the breath return to whatever feels natural.
3. Observe how you feel in your body and mind right now.
4. When you're ready, bring someone to mind whom you find challenging. You might want to start with a relatively neutral or slightly difficult person rather than picking the most challenging person you know.
5. Do your best to let go of the reasons why this person is difficult and just focus on the person themselves.
6. As you picture this person, take a moment to consider what makes you both human. Just like you, they feel pain and pleasure, they struggle, and they feel lost and insecure at times.
7. Say to yourself:

   "This person has feelings, thoughts, a body, and a mind—just like me."

   "This person is doing their best—just like me."

"This person makes mistakes—just like me."

"This person wants to be happy—just like me."

You can make up phrases that feel appropriate for you, focusing on what you share with this person, not what divides you.

Notice how these connections make this person more three-dimensional in your mind and heart. Instead of being a "bad guy," you now see someone who is human, just like you—someone who, just like you, deserves compassion and understanding, even if they continue to be difficult.

Applying the Practice

It's likely you don't have to think very hard to come up with someone for this exercise. Use this technique before you have a meeting with that person in your office or when you go to your in-laws' house for the holidays. It's also helpful to use this practice with your children when things are challenging. When your kid slams the door in your face, remember that you probably did the same thing to your parents and think, "Just like me, they are having a rough day."

Sharing with Kids

As kids struggle with cliques, wayward friends, or romances that turn sour, do this practice with them. This exercise is helpful when they are frustrated with a teacher who is "unfair" or when a friend or sibling invokes an "I hate you," door-slamming reaction. Encouraging your kids to focus on similarities can also be a really valuable lesson to share when they encounter someone who looks different than they do, perhaps someone who is homeless, smells "funny," or speaks a different language.

Common Obstacles

It's helpful to understand that this exercise isn't about letting people walk all over you or forgiving unforgivable actions. This technique is not actually about them at all—it's for you. You decide to see this person in a different light so you can let go of your own anger or frustration. The person might still be difficult, but you choose to change your perspective because that anger or frustration ultimately impacts only you.

Practice: Open Awareness Meditation

This practice is similar to the One-Minute Breath Meditation (page 20) except that instead of staying with one focus, or breath, we allow our awareness to be broader, taking in whatever is alive in the moment.

1. Start with a few deep breaths as a signal that this is a break from your usual mode and a time for yourself to sit and be with what's happening. Remember, as we discussed in the 5-4-3-2-1 Grounding practice (page 51), a deep breath signals to your brain that you are safe.
2. Let the breath return to normal.
3. Stay with the narrower focus on the breath for just a few moments, using it to settle your attention wherever possible.
4. Then let the focus be broader. What's most obvious in your awareness right now? It might be a physical sensation, an emotion, a sound—any stimulus at all is appropriate.
5. Explore the stimulus with kind, curious attention. See how it changes, explore where it starts and ends. What does it feel like in your body?
6. The stimulus might feel really nice (a cool breeze or feeling of relaxation) or decidedly unpleasant (back pain or anger, for example). See if you can be with it just as it is, regardless of your judgment of it.

7. This exercise is not about making anything happen or about changing the experience. Just notice and see if you can be in the moment with patience and compassion.

8. When that experience dissipates, you can end the practice or move on to a new focus.

Applying the Practice

Stop at any moment. What is happening right now? What are you most aware of? This technique hones your attention as well as your patience because you learn to be with things as they are, and it lets you accept the challenging parenting moments as well as the sweet ones. This exercise can also keep you focused on your kids when your mind starts to wander.

Sharing with Kids

Kids are great at this. Use the image of a microscope (narrow focus) and satellite (broad focus). Have them turn the "beam" to different parts of the room or to their bodies. What do they notice? This activity is also really useful in helping them see that they're in charge of which parts of their experience they see most clearly.

Common Obstacles

The challenge here is wanting this moment to be different than it is. It's hard to be kind and curious with something we habitually don't like. Yet that's where the biggest changes can happen. Try to explore something like knee pain or frustrated feelings as if it were happening to someone else so you don't have to take it personally.

Practice: Every Moment Is a Teacher

This practice is all about changing how we relate to difficulty. We get to pause, see our usual patterns (sense of urgency, yelling, blaming others, or berating ourselves) and choose kindness and space instead.

1. First, breathe. Breathing is the best way to make yourself pause, breaking the momentum of whatever story your mind is telling you.
2. Notice how your body feels in this moment. Feel your breath going in and out, the air on your skin, the temperature of your hands. Notice any sounds that are present.
3. Check in with your present state. If you are impatient, notice what impatient feels like. Give the feeling a name as in Name That Emotion (page 59). If you're anxious or angry, notice what the emotion feels like in your body.
4. Ask yourself, "What's happening right now? How am I relating to what's happening?"

5. Chances are that what's happening is out of your control. But you can change how you are relating to it by being kind, curious, nonjudgmental, and mindful.

6. If you see that you are resisting this moment or fighting it, see if you can soften your whole body and mind. Do this by taking a few deep breaths and consciously relaxing.

7. Remind yourself that being angry won't make the kids quieter, for example. Anger just makes you more stressed.

8. You can ask yourself, "How do I want to be in this moment?" or "Is this actually helping me right now?"

9. Instead of fighting or resisting this moment, think about what you can learn from it and what the struggle you are experiencing is trying to teach you.

Applying the Practice

If you find yourself freaking out because you can't find your keys, your work has been criticized, or you feel overwhelmed with housework, see if you can shift your perspective through this practice. It's empowering to notice when you're going down an unhelpful road and then choose if you want to stay on that path. Mindfulness lets us be the ones in charge of how we are in any given moment. Use this technique for those challenging parenting situations like when you can't find parking at the mall, when everyone is arguing, when your kids won't eat the food that was their favorite yesterday, or when you just can't figure out what to do for dinner. (In a way, we can thank our kids for challenging us so much because they give us so many opportunities to practice patience.)

Sharing with Kids

Kids, like us, get caught up in emotions, narratives, and their expectations about the way things should go. Share this exercise as you are doing it, so they can see this tool in action. You might offer a practice run where you imagine a difficult scenario and picture yourself stopping and exploring how you want to be before you get upset. Use characters in their books and ask your kids to brainstorm more helpful ways that character could respond. Or ask, "What do you think they are feeling in their bodies right now? What else could they do besides run away?"

Common Obstacles

Life is still going to be hard, and kids are still going to misbehave. Just because you practice mindfulness doesn't mean everything will feel great. The purpose is to focus on the intention to pause and change your perspective. Even if you can't completely change how you see a situation, the attempt is enough to give you space from your habitual responses and build more patience and compassion.

CHAPTER 7

BREAKING BAD HABITS OR NEGATIVE BEHAVIORS

One of the most humbling things about raising my daughter is realizing how many habits I have that I don't want to pass on to her. From patterns related to important issues, like body image, to mundane tendencies, like how often I play with my hair, my daughter's impressionable presence has made me hyperaware of several not-so-great habits that I've been unconsciously practicing for years.

Mindfulness actually serves the same function in a way. At the beginning, mindfulness felt really rough because it seemed I was becoming mindful only of bad habits and all of the things I believed I was doing wrong. I focused on the negatives way more than the positives and had the habit of calling myself names whenever something went wrong.

Nevertheless, mindfulness was the necessary first step toward transformation. I couldn't change what I couldn't see. Practicing mindfulness let me see my patterns and then decide if I wanted to perpetuate them or find a new path.

Some of our negative habits aren't our fault. The tendency to see the bad more than the good is evolutionarily wired into all of us. A research group from Case Western Reserve University discovered that bad ideas, challenging events, and difficult memories have more impact on us, stick in our brains more, and get stored more easily in our memories than positive ones do. Scientists call it the negativity bias. You might call it the parent-teacher interview effect. The teacher spends 10 minutes saying how lovely your child is, how much they've improved, and how well they get along with their classmates. Then the teacher adds that your child needs a bit of work with discipline. What's the one thing that sticks in your mind?

Mindfulness gives us the tools to (1) recognize our patterns, (2) compassionately, kindly explore how we are thinking and feeling without blaming ourselves—while still being accountable for mistakes we've made—and (3) decide to continue this way or change based on how our patterns make us feel. Going back to the metaphor of the mind as a garden, we get to decide which seeds we plant and which weeds we pull. If I can see that I'm stuck on a negative comment, I can recognize my focus, then choose to stop feeding that negative voice and turn my attention to the positive, supportive, kind, and helpful moments. And this works for any habit we might want to break: nail biting, mindless snacking, not listening, getting frustrated with teenagers. Mindfulness also helps us see that beating ourselves up about our patterns doesn't actually help at all (it's just another bad habit we might be stuck in).

Mindfulness isn't about telling you how to live your life or what habits to keep and what habits to drop. Mindfulness is about empowering each of us to have more of a say in how we are living the lives we have.

Practice: Sending Kind Wishes

The purposeful cultivation of helpful qualities and thoughts helps us break common, ingrained habits, like judging others, feeling jealous, or being hard on ourselves. Here, we wish others and ourselves kind thoughts as a way of planting helpful seeds.

1. Take a few deep breaths and feel your body exactly how it is.
2. Breathing normally, bring to mind someone that makes you happy or someone you love.
3. Really picture this person—imagine putting a smile on their face or having them laugh with you. Notice how this person makes you feel as you focus on them in your mind.
4. Think about all of the good things you would wish for this person.

5. Send this person kind thoughts by saying these phrases (or making up your own):

"I wish for you to be happy."
"I wish you for you to feel good."
"I wish for you to feel love."

6. Imagine this person can really feel your good wishes.
7. Depending on how much time you have, you might focus on just that one person or you might choose to extend these kind wishes to others and to yourself. You can include family members, friends, work associates, or people you see often but don't know, like a bus driver or a postal worker. You can even send kind thoughts to someone who is difficult in your life.
8. Before you finish, make sure to take a moment or two to send kind thoughts to yourself: "I wish to be happy. I wish to be peaceful."

Applying the Practice

Use this exercise as an antidote to judgmental patterns. Instead of "I'm an idiot," try "I made a mistake. I'm human. I wish for myself to be happy." Part of this technique involves paying attention to self-talk (yours and your kids') and responding with more supportive words.

It's a surprisingly powerful practice to send good wishes to anyone any time you can. To the person you pass in your car, to the person who is slow at the checkout line, to the parent in your kid's class who never volunteers: "I wish for you to be happy." The more kind wishes you cultivate, the more you will feel.

Sharing with Kids

This exercise demonstrates to us and to our kids that we have the power to choose our thoughts and to direct our intentions. It's a beautiful practice to make part of a bedtime routine, connecting to kindness and good wishes for others. You can each pick someone new to send kind wishes to each night. Encourage children to send kind thoughts to teachers or other adults they might not see as real people. This practice helps kids learn to respond with kindness instead of anger or depersonalization.

Common Obstacles

It can be most challenging to send kind thoughts to yourself. If it feels difficult, see if you can be gentle with yourself, perhaps practicing some self-compassion (page 86). It also might feel silly, forced, or weird, and that's okay. Like making ourselves smile, sending ourselves well-wishes might feel strange, but it does make us feel better.

Practice: Self-Compassion

Self-criticism is one of the most destructive and diffi-cult habits to change. Self-compassion and its three components—kindness, mindfulness, and common humanity—are ways to see our struggles in a new light.

1. As always, take a breath or two. Notice how your cur-rent emotions feel in your body.
2. Perhaps take a moment to give yourself heartfelt permission to do this practice. Remember you're doing this for a reason, and it's fine to feel however you feel.
3. It's helpful to begin with a One-Minute Breath Meditation (page 20) or Body Scan (page 10). Exercises like those give you a chance to let go of what's occupying your mind so that you can come back to the present moment and your intentions for self-compassion.
4. Connect to your wish to feel more peaceful or to be kinder to yourself. Imagine you could breathe in kind-ness and compassion as you inhale.
5. In your mind, offer yourself the phrases below (or ones you create for yourself):

Kindness

- "I'm okay."
- "I don't have to solve this right now."
- "I wish to be peaceful."
- "I love myself."

Mindfulness

- "I'm really suffering right now."
- "This is really hard."
- "I'm feeling lost in this moment."
- "This hurts."

Common Humanity

- "I'm not alone."
- "There is nothing wrong with me."
- "Other people feel this way, too."

6. Repeat these phrases to yourself as much as you need or have time for.
7. As you finish, imagine someone who loves you or someone you truly love giving you a big hug, stroking your hair, or telling you it's okay. Let yourself feel held and supported.
8. Take a few more deep breaths.

Applying the Practice

Self-compassion isn't about getting rid of painful feelings. The goal is to be kind and gentle to ourselves, just as we are, while things are hard. Try to come up with two or three go-to phrases that you can remember, write down, and have ready when you need them. You might use phrases you regularly share with your kids, like "I love you to the moon and back."

It can be particularly challenging for caregivers to give ourselves compassion when we're so used to caring for others. Consider how you would talk to your children or partner if they were feeling this way. Anytime you notice you want to call yourself a bad parent or judge how you are doing, see if you can turn to self-compassion instead.

Sharing with Kids

When your children are down or dealing with challenges, encourage them to remember that's it's okay to feel however they feel (rather than you or them trying to change it or solve it immediately). Ask them how they would treat a friend (or a stuffed animal) if they were going through this right now or what they would say to a character in a book who was feeling down.

Common Obstacles

It's hardest to be self-compassionate when you need it most. Remind yourself that you're doing this exercise for a reason, that it's important to care for yourself right now, and it's all right to be scared, confused, or not have any answers.

At times, this practice can feel false or even make you feel a bit worse because you are turning toward the feelings instead of away from them. Know that however you feel is right. Try to trust and explore this exercise, regardless of how it feels at the time.

Practice: Five Good Things for Every Bad One

Marriage counsellor Dr. John Gottman found that content couples have five positive interactions for every negative one. The following practice applies that important research to our parenting and familial relationships, so that we can mindfully combat the negativity bias inherent in all of us. Use this practice whenever you feel stuck in negative thinking or any other habit you'd like to change.

1. Take a few deep breaths. Notice where you are and what your body feels like right now.
2. Acknowledge the unhelpful habit with gentle awareness. Whether you're judging yourself or someone else, calling yourself names, or yelling at the dog, take a moment to notice what's happening. Revisit your intention to choose a kinder response.
3. Look for counterexamples. If you're stuck on all the times you've fought with your 13-year-old, remember (even write down) several times when you connected and commit to making those times happen in a similar way in the near future.
4. Notice how connecting to this positive, alternative way of seeing feels in your mind and body.
5. Take a few more deep breaths.
6. Finally, thank yourself for seeing the habit and choosing an alternative that promotes well-being for you and your loved ones. That gratitude reinforces this practice.

Applying the Practice

With mindfulness, you'll likely become increasingly aware of negative self-talk. Each time you notice you've been self-deprecating or judgmental, try to come up with five things that counter that thought or remember five times where you were—or even tried to be—mindful, kind, aware, or patient.

You can use this for physical or lifestyle habits, too. If you notice you've been feeling road rage, take care to notice times when you've been calmer in the car (or make those five times happen). If the weather is getting you down, look through pictures for those times when you enjoyed being outside.

Sharing with Kids

Start a "Good Things" journal with your children (writing things down offers another way to emphasize them in your mind). You can make this a craft project and decorate journals as a family.

Try to incorporate this practice regularly. When someone says, "School sucks" or "I'm terrible at hockey," brainstorm counterexamples together. Make an effort to do this together after a family argument.

It's important to allow feelings to be felt before trying to address other ways of seeing the situation. When your preteen says, "I hate my sister," give her the space to feel that hurt or anger. When she's ready, you might encourage her gently to consider times she and her sister got along.

Common Obstacles

Our brains are so much better at seeing and remembering the negative than the positive, which makes this exercise tricky. But if you know that tendency exists, you don't have to blame yourself for it. You can even name it aloud: "This is just negativity bias. I'm going to train my brain the way I want."

If you can't think of any positive examples in the moment, that's fine. That can happen if your brain is in an activated state. You might try a One-Minute Breath Meditation (page 20) or 5-4-3-2-1 Grounding practice (page 51) before you come back to this.

CHAPTER 8

WHERE TO MINDFULLY GO FROM HERE

After six-and-a-half years of being a parent, making a million mistakes, seeing my daughter grow and change, figuring out how to get her to stay in bed at night (admittedly still working on that one), talking to other parents, and reading about parenting, two things are certain. First, there is no word funnier than *poop* when you're six years old. And second, there are no perfect parents and no perfect kids—just perfect moments. Mine include drawing shapes on my daughter's back and our family cuddling in bed, making up silly songs together and getting filthy splashing in puddles, watching her master those (dreaded) monkey bars, and her making me "soup" when I was sick.

What makes these moments perfect isn't that they are 100 percent happy or photo-album worthy. They're perfect because everyone is present, allowing the moment to be just how it is. Mindfulness doesn't make all the moments perfect. Instead, it helps us enjoy and be present for the moments we can and be gentle with ourselves for those that are challenging.

The key here is to make mindfulness a regular part of your life. Then it's not yet another thing to do—it's just the way things are. By reading this book, you are choosing a more supportive, healthy way of being with yourself and your children. Being mindful isn't always easy, but it is worth it.

Sadly, this book can't do the work for you. You schlep your kids to soccer, piano, karate, and circus classes so they can practice. Like them, you, too, have to practice. You have to keep coming back to your breath, your body, and the moment just as it is, with kindness and curiosity. The more you practice mindfulness, the more natural it becomes, the more it becomes part of who you are and how you see the world and yourself in it.

So how do you bring mindfulness into your everyday life in a real and doable way?

These are the three main takeaways for making mindfulness habitual:

1. Create routines.
2. Practice many short moments of awareness of your body and senses.
3. Make being mindful interesting and fun.

1. Create Routines

Use the practices in the book (or create your own) to build a routine that fits for you. You might ask your children what made them grateful today at bedtime, have a mindful hug and breath before you leave in the morning, or set aside time once a week for a family sensory walk. Routines don't need to be elaborate or lengthy. The more you build mindfulness into your everyday life, the easier it is. Be creative and also trust that practicing mindfulness can be as simple as one breath at a particular time or place.

While it's important to have your own routines, it's also sweet to let your kids take the lead. Let them choose how to begin a meal mindfully. Maybe you take a few deep breaths or you just listen to the sounds in the room. Perhaps the ritual concludes with family members bestowing upon one another unicorn horns, vampire capes, or other magical powers (as is the case with the ever-evolving ritual in our house). The details of the ritual are beside the point. The key is to sit, breathe, and connect to the present moment together.

Here are some other ways you can build rituals:

- On a family walk or in the backyard, choose a stone. Keep the stone in your pocket as a reminder to breathe or pause when you need it. Each morning, you might clink stones or just hold them while you take a breath together.

- Create a mindful space in the house or apartment. This can be the corner of a room or just a special pillow facing a different way. You might use candles (if appropriate), pictures, crystals, or stones. Make it a place you and your family choose to seek out if they need to take a breath and just be.

- You and your partner or a friend might text each other once a day with a simple message: "Breathe," "Pause," or "Kindness." Rituals like this help us stay accountable and remind us to come back to the present.

- Create a morning ritual for yourself to reconnect with your intentions for and commitment to this way of being. Before you check your phone or even get out of bed, take a deep breath and remind yourself why you wanted to practice mindfulness in the first place. Here are some suggestions: "I am choosing to be more present for my kids," "I wish to be kinder to myself," or "I'm doing this so I can really enjoy the moment."

2. Practice Many Short Moments of Awareness of Your Body and Senses

Practicing short moments of awareness is the suggestion that makes mindfulness doable for busy parents. It's not the duration of your mindful practice that's important, but rather how many times a day you can notice what's happening and be with it in a kind, curious, nonjudgmental manner. Just one breath over and over again makes your mindfulness practice stick. Connect to the senses and the breath so you get a break from your busy mind and return to the here and now.

Here are some other suggestions for short moments of sensory awareness:

- Use the changing seasons or weather as a cue to check in. You can notice snow falling, waves crashing, trees blooming. Feel the raindrops on your skin. Set a ritual of stopping for a moment and noticing the air on your skin before you commute to work.

- Use a moment of giggling with kids to connect to this moment, your body, and them.

- Pick anything you encounter on a regular basis and make that your reminder to pause and take a breath. You can use a red traffic light, a phone ringing, the neighbor's dog barking—anything that might help you remember to find one more moment of awareness in your day. You can even pick something as a family or a couple, so you have your mindful moment together.

- Touch is so powerful here. It's soothing for kids and adults and helps us connect to the moment. Play "Guess What Shape I'm Drawing" on each other's backs or arms. This game builds connection and anchors everyone involved to the present moment by encouraging attention to the sensations. (An activity that involves touch is also an excellent tool when you are waiting for a music lesson or at the dentist and your children start to get fidgety.)

3. Make Being Mindful Fun and Enjoyable

You already have too many things to do. You don't need another thing to take too seriously or to feel bad about neglecting. So approach mindfulness with humor and a light touch.

Here are some suggestions for making mindfulness fun:

- Let your kids take the lead. As they play with Legos or in a sandbox, ask them to notice colors or the feel of the sand on their skin. For adolescents, ask to listen to their preferred style of music. You don't have to like it but see if you can just enjoy their enjoyment.

- Use mindfulness as an opportunity to look at the stars, try weird-looking foods, or make up silly dances.

- One of the best unintentionally mindful activities I've ever done was playing with slime. You know that homemade goopy stuff you can put together with ingredients you have around the house? It's remarkably fun to touch, play with, hold, and manipulate. It was silly and wonderful.

- Find something you enjoy and notice how it makes you feel. Maybe you and your partner decide to feed each other chocolate or go to a wine tasting and go overboard with your sommelier sniffing act.

- Don't worry about getting it right and don't forget to laugh at how hard it is to just sit and pay attention.

And if all else fails, just remember this:

1. Breathe.
2. Choose kindness.
3. Repeat.

SUGGESTED RESOURCES

Books

Mindfulness: An Eight-Week Plan for Finding Peace in a Frantic World by Mark Williams and Danny Penman

The Mindful Teen: Powerful Skills to Help You Handle Stress One Moment at a Time by Dzung X. Vo

The Mindful Way through Depression: Freeing Yourself from Chronic Unhappiness by Mark Williams, John Teasdale, Zindel V. Segal, and Jon Kabat-Zinn

The Whole-Brain Child: 12 Revolutionary Strategies to Nurture Your Child's Developing Mind by Daniel J. Siegel and Tina Payne Bryson

Wherever You Go, There You Are: Mindfulness Meditation in Everyday Life by Jon Kabat-Zinn

Websites

Child Honouring: www.raffifoundation.org/take-the-course

Embodied Wisdom: www.mbodiedwisdom.com

Follow Your Breath: www.followyourbreath.com

Rick Hanson: www.rickhanson.net

Self-Compassion: www.self-compassion.org

University of California, San Diego Center for Mindfulness: health.ucsd.edu/specialties/mindfulness/Pages/default.aspx

University of Massachusetts Medical School Center for Mindfulness: www.umassmed.edu/cfm/mindfulness-based -programs

Children's Books

Anh's Anger by Gail Silver

Charlotte and the Quiet Place by Deborah Sosin

Even Superheroes Have Bad Days by Shelly Becker

My Many Colored Days by Dr. Seuss

Peaceful Piggy Meditation by Kerry Lee MacLean

Steps and Stones by Gail Silver

Sticky Brains by Nicole Libin

REFERENCES

Baumeister, Roy F., Ellen Bratslavsky, Catrin Finkenauer, and
Kathleen D. Vohs. "Bad Is Stronger Than Good." *Review of
General Psychology*, 5, no. 4 (2001): 323-370. https://doi.org
/10.1037/1089-2680.5.4.323.

Benson, Kyle. "The Magic Relationship Ratio, According to
Science." *The Gottman Institute*. October 4, 2017. https://
www.gottman.com/blog/the-magic-relationship-ratio
-according-science/.

Glasper, Erica R. and Gretchen N. Neigh. "Editorial: Experience-
Dependent Neuroplasticity Across the Lifespan: From Risk to
Resilience." *Frontiers in Behavioral Neuroscience* 12 (2019): 335.
https://doi.org/10.3389/fnbeh.2018.00335.

Gottman, John, Julie Schwartz Gottman, and Joan Declaire.
*Ten Lessons to Transform Your Marriage: America's Love
Lab Experts Share Their Strategies for Strengthening Your
Relationship*. New York: Three Rivers Press, 2006.

Gottman, John, and Nan Silver. *The Seven Principles for Making
Marriage Work: A Practical Guide from the Country's Foremost
Relationship Expert*. New York: Three Rivers Press, 1999.

Ireland, Tom. "What Does Mindfulness Meditation Do to Your
Brain?" *Scientific American*. June 12, 2014. https://blogs
.scientificamerican.com/guest-blog/what-does-mindfulness
-meditation-do-to-your-brain/.

Taren, Adrienne A., J. David Creswell, and Peter J. Gianaros. "Dispositional Mindfulness Co-Varies with Smaller Amygdala and Caudate Volumes in Community Adults." *PLOS ONE* 8, no. 5 (2013): e64574. https://doi.org/10.1371/journal.pone.0064574.

PRACTICES INDEX

INDEX